T0157474

OVERCOMER

Wisdom & Light Quotes

S TEPHANA P EA

OVERCOMER
WISDOM & LIGHT QUOTES

iUniverse books may be ordered through booksellers or by contacting:

iUniverse
1663 Liberty Drive
Bloomington, IN 47403
www.iuniverse.com
1-800-Authors (1-800-288-4677)

ISBN: 978-1-5320-9582-5 (sc)
ISBN: 978-1-5320-9581-8 (e)

Library of Congress Control Number: 2020903405

Print information available on the last page.

iUniverse rev. date: 02/28/2020

When wisdom is necessary to our daily lives
When knowledge empowers us
And when experience is our Teacher

Wisdom & Light
Visit our Instagram Page: wisdom2Light

Preface

This book is a self-help and self-improvement book a result of attending so many conferences, seminars and be able to follow some leaders and also be inspire by their actions.

Wisdom and Light book is a citation book that will encourage and motivate you on your daily life. It is a book that will build you mentally and make you even stronger.

Wisdom and Light is a daily inspiration of everyday challenges. You will learn, be transform and change forever.

A life without challenges is meaningless and when wisdom is crucial in our decisions

Wisdom is a path to the light and being Enlighted is only when you are conscious.

Conscious about your life, spirituality, and stay firm in your tough moments.

Wisdom and Light is a book where I was too much confronted with decisions and I have made a lot of mistakes in the past. Which has led me to "Wisdom". We all have our past, a darkness part of us, where is hidden and we do not know people to notice. Nobody is perfect, in addition, we learn from nature, we learn from our community and society.

However, wisdom brings wealth. Many people want to build wealth, but they neglecting the small things in their life. Start with the little you have had, develop it.

'' Every day with wisdom and light". I have started being aware of my days. I will write down anything that crossed my mind and captured my attention. Whether I was doing something, I do it with a purpose, and since I am a continuous learning human being who are thirsty about knowledge, the universe, nature. You need wisdom, light because we are divine and totally connected to our creator.

Wisdom will hep you take great decisions as a fool man or woman. When you are a fool learn from those who are wise, observe, a speak less. For example, imagine You are among successful man or woman, we will become the next target even if you are not smart enough. Wisdom helps you walk, not only walk out of the pit. But, you will be aware of where are going, and why? There was a man in the bible who was wise and gain honor and wealth king Solomon. King Solomon became wealthy which shows us that we can multiply what we have (talents &skills). Wisdom helps you to the understanding of yourself. You do not live until you understood yourself.

Use your gifts, talents and skills wisely. Let your light shine.

You are an overcomer
You can
You have already won your Battle
You have a strong mind
You are a light
You are created for good purpose
You are wise

Finally, wisdom is better than folly, just as light is better than Darkness

Wisdom2Light citations

Without discipline, you
won't be successful

———◆———

Do not let the problem
demoralize you

———◆———

You are in charge of your
life. Be the pilot

Ignorance will keep you enslaved

When you are with a wise
man you will become wiser

Discussion forces you to go further

Money can't buy happiness

The mistakes of the past are
great lessons to better advance
and plan the future

The mistakes of the past
are source of blessings to be
able to discover yourself

Having a vision of what we want is very important because it will lead you to achieve them, make them happen

———◆———

Get up and follow your dreams

———◆———

Every obstacle is a hidden wisdom

God has gifted each of us with

something Unique and different

The gift of sharing is so

important and useful

---

the strongest Men were first weakest

Trials make you stronger

and you gain wisdom

***

Your Failure becomes a success for

you when you decide to change

***

Self-Knowledge is also

knowing who you truly are

Open your eyes and decide

to shine today

Dare to dream again and again

Joyfully accept a hidden rebuke

Better a sincere friendship

than pretending to love

———◆———

He who reflects on things

finds happiness

———◆———

Knowledge is Better than Wealth

Don't be afraid to be rejected by people, they should love you for who you are, not what you have

———◆———

Stop being too emotional and sensitive, the world belongs to those who are much stronger enough to challenge themselves

———◆———

God's plan is the best one

Your harvest time is yet to come

When Life stings or tough, be Brave

Love is not obtained by
force, nor by negotiation

You don't need to prove anything,
time will surely do it

Some genius men have had learning
disabilities which never prevent
them from impacting the world

A Silence is not Synonym
of ignorance

Don't talk, start doing

You were born to shine

Knowledge is wealth

Wisdom is much better than Gold

Enlightment is the path to the truth

Ignorance is one of the
devil's favorite weapons

Complicated problems

have simple solutions

Don't look for a treasure,

Be the Treasure

Don't lose hope when

you lose Something

If Life puts you down don't cry

just be ready to challenge

You are a Queen, you

deserve what is better

Yes, you can make it

Failure is the beginning

of your Success

You are the one who sees

the vision, Believe it

Everything in this world is Broken

If you can battle, then you can win

Start over, over again

Don't get distracted, follow
your dreams, your passions

Perseverance leads to success

The Secret of Perseverance
leads to success

The Key to a happy life is to
create your life plan and submit
it to God, incorporate the
suggested changes, and live your
life according to God's plan

A Life without obstacles,

without problems is not life

Individuals are banks savers

Great Leaders are also great listeners

Even the weak can still

become strong

When you find a love one, a

true love never let her go

True love is real and does exist

Man has the ability to create things

Fear is our worst enemy (the

enemy of that limit Man)

Our first enemy is ourselves

A leader is not like everyone.

He does things differently

The enemy of our own

destiny is often ourselves

Struggle and failure are not your final destination. It is a self-rediscovery of your direction

It takes an idea to put into action

Achievement is a self-satisfaction of your dreams that once was just a dream but turn into reality

It is better to start today, do
not wait until tomorrow

You earn your goals behind the
scene before the world sees it.
You are a champion, dig it.

Love what you do, and
hope in what you do

The smile hides the inner joys
and pains that no man can see

There is no faithful friend like a
book with it you learn so fast

A winner is a dreamer
who never gives up

Sensible people always

think before they act

———◆———

Books are best friends

———◆———

Reading broadens our mind

Don't carry big stones if you are
not ready to carry small ones

You can't tell your friends all your
secrets, they can use it against
you. Be careful who you trust

A truth worthy friend is often loyal

Don't stop educating yourself.
You are the product of your
results and actions

When you don't know your enemies,
it is difficult to fight & win the battle

He who never lose will never
know or understands the
concept of winning or losing

People you consider friends can
instantly become your worst
enemies. Don't hurt people

Your Heart is not a place of sadness
Armed soldier is never afraid of death

There is nothing stronger than
seeing loved ones happy

If only you believe you can

do impossible things

———◆———

Every problem has a solution

Death is natural

———◆———

Positive attitude is nurturing

and contagious

Words are powerful and eternal

The only weapon to use

against your enemies is Love.

Love with all your heart

Education is better than riches

A worker is not a Slave

It is better to advise and be wise
when you practice your words

A hero is hidden in you, you are a
man and a woman of distinction

The Dirt builds your character

I Dare you to dream

There is a Gold in You.

Do not give up

A Positive attitude creates

more miracles

Truth without Love is Hypocrisy

When we do believe in ourselves

truly good things start to happen

Every obstacle presents

an opportunity to improve

one's condition

Climbing to the top is not

easy, but not impossible

Perseverance is the key

to achievement

Leader are also great observers

Don't be a quitter, it is not
in your blood DNA

Inner fear will only limit you
to reach higher/prevents you
on reaching your goals

This is not every question that
necessarily requires an answer

Criticism is an opportunity to
better improve or change yourself
Betrayal is your closest friend when
you don't know who to trust

Jealousy is the witchcraft of a
person who has a wicked Heart

Truth will always set you free

Life is a continuous learning process

Don't let yourself be
controlled by a friend

Money is the root of all Evil

True wisdom comes from God

Gold does not seek its value

Words that lead to life come

out of the wise man's mouth

Learn by doing and take Action

Failing is another chance of doing

better and becoming better

Good things never come without
you getting into action

#Shine, shine, "Brighter"

Transformation is like a superpower

Wisdom is very precious

Be Patient in your seed

Always set your priorities

Without a clear vision and a plan you cannot accomplish your goals

Knowledge is non-physical asset. No one can take it from you

Don't be jealous of other people's success, instead learn from them

You cannot achieve great things if

you are entitled with old mentality

Stay Positive and write

down your dreams

Work daily on yourself before you

desiring to change the world

Training is the one of the steps
to your dreams' fulfillment

Have friends who are willing
to support you, be there for
you when you are in need

Climb your mountains very high
and don't look backward

Be grateful to the people who
did not believe in YOU, for you
had to believe in yourself

The only weapon you can use
against your enemies is LOVE

Love is not about words,
True love is action

Don't tell me about you, let

me define who you are

———◆———

If you want to succeed, Work

hard, but even harder

———◆———

When Life is unfair, then you

bring the mood out of it

Humility brings the blessing

Humility is not stupidity

We are uniquely gifted, we have
different battles and destiny

Persistent is the true art
of achievement without it
no one can succeed

It does not matter if you
failed yesterday. Today is a
new day. Start all over

Sometimes playing a fool is better
than showing how smart you are

Do not accuse people for

your own failures

If you want it so bad, work for it

Life without a purpose is meaningless

A Man without a vision

is a death-Man

Without a clear vision, no

one can achieve anything

Self-improvement is the best

investment ever in your life

Self-management is important,

master thyself and people

When you know your identity, it

is easier to make great decisions

"Knowing who you are"

Any situation in life is not eternal

Have a poor mind without
action. You will remain poor

Knowledge is the best ever
investment which cannot
be taken from you

your Brand is "you", it is your word

Be like a diamond, be rare, be unique, then the world will find you

---

Don't you hide your God's given gifts

Develop your gifts,

"become better at it"

Even if you are not proud where you

are today, there is a second chance.

A chance to do better, a chance to

get where you have always dreamed

off, a chance to push yourself up.

Those who doubt you, motivate you

You win your crown in the secret.

So, learn to appreciate every

single step of your journey

———◆———

your past mistakes are a stepping

stone to a great change

———◆———

Your Million ideas would

make you rich

It takes a simple idea for you

to develop and become rich

People don't want you, when

you die they know your worth

You can be busy, still not effective

Sometimes Less is not laziness

Give up on self-doubt,

insecurity and fear

The greatest investment you

can do is to invest in thyself

"Be Good, be better, be
great" in all you do

Stepping out of your comfort
zones is a path to success,
with learn from others too

Knowing or not knowing we should
ask ourselves some questions

A small peptalk on the daily
basis will motivate you, be
your own booster, boost your
mind and self-confidence

———————◆———————

Don't just be a good talker,
be a good doer

———————◆———————

Talker don't do anything in life.
They like to boast and pride

Be loyal to yourself

Never lower your standards in order
to make someone's else happy

Personal improvement comes first
before you desire to change the world

Don't be afraid to let yourself

shine, shine like a sun

Start now, build your future

What you choose, what to focus

on depends on your perception

The only thing prevailing
you to achieve your goals is
yourself "Speak, thought"

Big responsibilities require
huge commitments

You cannot change your life without
changing first your mentality

Being private is better

than being none

People can destroy your

reputation, when they have

more information about you

Privacy is everything. It is not

because you are not sharing about

your lifestyle. You're out date.

Don't ever lower your standards
to make anyone's happy. Go
higher, keep running your own
Race and stay true to yourself

They want you to follow
them. I am not a follower

Talk less about yourself. This
is another sign of Humility

You will not know someone by their face only, but by their heart as well

Can you save one and kill thousand? Will you save thousands and kill one? You will save both one and Thousands

The beauty of life is to love unconditionally

A Man with big heart will win
others and can become a Leader

Loving the creator and others
with all your heart, just as
yourself. This is the true faith

All the criticisms, you have gone
through used it to build your
empire and better yourself

Do you know how it felt

to be treated unfairly

If you can ask good questions,

then you can have right answers

Imagination is also creativity

Always try new things

some people's experiences are
not the same as your experience,
and it is not even your destiny

Sometimes, when people are against

your success, Prove them wrong

Cut yourself off from

toxic relationships

Help others, but don't try

to be like God to them

When people reject you,

be happy and rejoice!

———◆———

Your skills and your talents

can help you earn your life

———◆———

Powerful minds birthed

powerful destiny

Be a Man of Excellence

In order to receive, you shall give...

Never underestimate yourself

Eagles fly only with eagles

True happiness starts from the inside

A positive attitude is contagious

and a negative one is toxic

If they are not willing to teach

you, learn from yourself

Friendship is like a golden treasure
you never want to miss someone
who make your life special.

Every Man on this earth are
searching for money, power
and to be famous. Fewer are
looking for the truth

Let people critize you, the more they
do it they are become even better

Sometimes, our first enemy

of life is ''ourselves''

———◆———

Your story is your crown "so, don't

be afraid or ashamed about it"

———◆———

Fake people are around us,

very few are loyal and true

Be a productive woman,

be independent

Don't waste your life, do something

with it, work- walk with purpose

Don't be too proud, there

are always people out there

who will better than you

Be a woman of Vision,

cultivate yourself

Love is about giving, love is

sacrifice, love is not taking

You are the giver of life

"you born to impact"

Some people disrespect you,

because you are broke"

When you have more resources.

People give you Respect

Do the right choices, so

you'll never regret later

You were born to serve

yourself and serve others

———————◆———————

All humans are valuable

———————◆———————

To build your Future, don't

be too distracted

Evaluate yourself, knowing
what did not work out for
you, then Start over again

Some people don't want to
see us become successful

You cannot build a house without
the right or good foundation

The hatred or rejection of people will never change your vision, stay focus

Your vision is personal

Never share your visions with people if you have not achieved yet

They do not like you, yet
they come to you

Try to become valuable if they
hate you, they won't hate your
gifts. Build yourself up

If you are willing to be more
knowledgeable, Be curious

Fight until you win, fight

for your generation, fight to

leave your legacy on Earth

Don't waste time, don't

waste your life

Work, work, work smart, work

hard to the point where you

are tired of your failure

Before you become so great,

think as you are one

Sometimes, it is Good to fail

Transformation does not happen

overnight, it is a process and

it requires a lot of work

Suffer today the pain of

discipline or regret it later

You are your own Hero

Some Leaders are hidden and

don't wear their crowns in the

public only in the secret

Sometimes, it is good to
keep your life private

If you never lose valuable things in
your life, you'll never know the value
of what you have and be thankful

Be my mentor, be my coach, be my
inspiration, be my role model, be
my Lead, let me follow your path by
finding my own Path. Teach me what
I do not know, and see me grow as a
fruit of your effort and investment

The idea you might have for your
business, someone's else has
one, develop it "Be unique"

Your level of understanding must
be greater than your competitors

We cry for thousand reasons. Crying
is necessary in certain stage of life

I can make it happen, I

can make it better

No one can change your life except

you alone. Write your story

Being a Fan is so cheap, so

many people have chosen it

Never sat and do nothing, at least

do something with your life

Be somewhere, be active

No step is too hard to overcome

Give yourself a push in

the right direction

Don't fear failure, fear

to win at all times

Walk out from things that limit you

There are people who will always sabotage your dreams. Be careful!

Wisdom, Knowledge and understanding equals Power

Never be satisfy of what you know you carry wisdom and just need to manifest

If you have no longer experience the worst in your life how will you appreciate the best. True Leaders are made through challenges

Life is meaningless without a purpose

It is better to try something than doing nothing at all

If your failure is not hurting
you, it means that you are
not yet ready for change

Those who become successful in life
are those who knows their potentials.
Knowing yourself and your talents.
Work on it until you make it

If no one wants to teach
you- teach yourself

If no one wants to encourage

you- Encourage yourself

If no one wants to support

you- Support yourself

If no one wants to believe in

you- Believe in yourself

Keep going, run your own
race, push yourself

———◆———

If you want to become successful
gain knowledge and wisdom. But
do work on your talents and skills

———◆———

Everyone wants to get the
crown without paying the
price# Nothing is Free

Success requires discipline

Your success will disturb certain
people because they can't see
you succeed in their eyes

Comparison is not your loyal friend.
Strong Focus on your Goals.

Education is the foundation of knowledge. Learn as much as you can

The only person you compete with Every day is 'YOU'

Printed in the United States
By Bookmasters